بسم الله الرحمن الرحيم

BUILD & ESTABLISH

A MODEL SOCIETY

بسم الله الرحمن الرحيم

BOOKLET

Copyright © 2019
WDM Publications LLC
All rights reserved.
First Edition

ISBN 9781086851366

بسم الله الرحمن الرحيم

CONTENTS

ACKNOWLEDGMENTS	IV
ABBREVIATIONS CLARIFIED	6
BUILD & ESTABLISH A MODEL SOCIETY	**7**
ABOUT THE AUTHOR	32

بسم الله الرحمن الرحيم

*In a 3-year period **Imam W. Deen Mohammed** led and oversaw the largest mass conversion to Islam in the history of the United States of America. He forged close ties with Muslim communities worldwide and established strong relationships with many of the world's faiths and their prominent leadership.*

***Imam W. Deen Mohammed**, leader of the largest community of Muslims in the United States of America passed on September 9, 2008. We pray that his work continues to grow and serve humanity as he would have desired it to, through all of us who have benefited so greatly from his teachings. Ameen*

Structure, Guard and Publish the Knowledge

"We need knowledge, then we need protection for it. How do you protect knowledge? Some people say, "You protect knowledge by not letting anybody interfere with it. Don't let anybody change it. Publish it! When you publish it, people know it. That's its protection." Yes! If you want to protect your knowledge, publish it! When you publish it, it is protected and the people know it. But if you keep it locked up to yourself, you will die, and your knowledge will die with you. Or your enemy will get a hold to it and he will publish it after you in a corrupt form.

Thus, Allah swt says. "And We have revealed it for the express purpose that it should be propagated." Yes! That is its guarantee that it will be protected. When it's propagated in its right form, then the people will inherit it directly. They don't have to listen to what you have to say. You won't have to tell them what Prophet Muhammad (pbuh) said, they got it directly. It was published by him in his lifetime.

If we want to guard the knowledge that we have, we must publish it. The more people know about it, the more it is guaranteed that it will live, and it won't be changed. The less people know about it, the better the chance that it will die with us or be changed. Yes! We structure the knowledge and we propagate the knowledge."
Imam W. Deen Mohammed

بسم الله الرحمن الرحيم

Abbreviations Clarified

G-d for God
In this book the word God is written as G-d for the respect of the word "god" because some people mirror to disrespect it with the word "dog."

swt for Subhana Wa Tallah
The abbreviation after Allah swt means "Subhana Wa Tallah" in Arabic which means "The Sacred and The Mighty" in English.

(PBUH) for Peace Be Upon Him
The abbreviation after Prophet Muhammad (pbuh) means "May the Peace and Blessings of Allah G-d be upon him" in English and "Sal Allahu Allahi Wa Salaam" in Arabic.

AS for Alayhi Salam
The abbreviation AS means "Alayhi Salaam" in Arabic, which means "May Allah G-d bless him" in English.

BUILD & ESTABLISH A MODEL SOCIETY

Jumuah Khutbah
Chicago, IL
October 19, 2001

بسم الله الرحمن الرحيم

Imam W. Deen Mohammed

Dear Believers, Peace Be Unto You, As Salaam-Alaikum. We praise Allah and witness that He is One, that He is the Creator of everything. He is the Lord of the heavens and the earth and cares about all of His creation. He created and then cared for His creation, until He brought this creation to guidance. The best of His creation is the servants of G-d, the Prophets, the Messengers of G-d. And He created man to be His servants and His Messengers.

That is fulfilled in the Prophets and Messengers of G-d and completed in Muhammed, The Prophet (pbuh), who is given to us as a model for our human and Muslim behavior. But not only is he given to us, Allah Most High says in His Book, the Qur'an, that whoever believes in G-d and the Last Day certainly has in Muhammed (pbuh), the most excellent model.

Again, Allah says of Muhammed the Prophet (pbuh) "We have not sent you to be other than a mercy to all the worlds." That means Muhammed (pbuh) came as a mercy to mankind, to all human beings. Not only to the individual, he came to the nations and to the institutions of the nations, to the learned and their most cherished establishments. Muhammed (pbuh) came as a mercy to them.

If you can give people correct knowledge and guide them to the sciences, the sciences of matter, you open the way for them to have comfort unlimited. When Allah says of Muhammed (pbuh), "We haven't sent you except as a mercy to all the worlds," that mercy Allah is speaking of is the second mercy. The Bible says that G-d promised the people who made covenant with Him that He would give them two portions of His Mercy.

بسم الله الرحمن الرحيم

Imam W. Deen Mohammed

In Islam, G-d is Ar-Rahman and Ar-Rahim. Two portions of His Mercy and Muhammed (pbuh) is a mercy to all the worlds, because it was the final revelation given to him, The Qur'an, that opened the minds of the scholars, of the scientists, the researchers, the thinking people to new and fresh doors for revival of the human intellect, with its rational powers and rational curiosities. And it gave birth to the revival of the sciences. This is history.

So we are not people just invited to rituals. We are invited to wake up in our sense nature, in our compassion and in our intelligence. We are guided in this religion to wake up in the best of our nature. We should be compassionate human beings and intelligent human beings and subscribe to the best human behavior. And we should respect as a people the best standards established in history by civilized man.

BUILD & ESTABLISH A MODEL SOCIETY

That is what Allah means, Highly Praised is He, when He says, "And order or give commands, instructions, respecting the best of standards established by civilized societies." It means that which is known as the best standards. And it continues, "Turn, keep away from that which empties out your good qualities and your good senses." This is the instruction of G-d.

We are addressing the importance of the human intellect. Muhammed the Prophet (pbuh) said, "G-d did not create anything more beneficial for us than the human intelligence." In fact, he said the human brain. I remember a sister who was very religious, who came from Catholicism to Islam, looking at me when I said that as if to say, "You are making a mistake, Brother Imam. The brain is not the most precious most beneficial thing G-d created."

بسم الله الرحمن الرحيم

Imam W. Deen Mohammed

I'm sure she was entertaining the heart as the most beneficial thing that G-d created.

Yes, the heart is first, and the brain is second. If we purify our heart, that is the door for the brain. The good condition of our heart stimulates the brain and gives the brain that kind of support it needs to stay straight and obedient to G-d. Yes, the heart is the first, but the heart has not given us electric lights as much as the brain has. You can want it in your heart all you want, but if you don't use your brain, you will never have electric lights and all the other things that make for an advanced and comfortable world.

So Muhammed the Prophet (pbuh) knew what he was saying, and he was correct. He said that G-d didn't create anything more useful or more beneficial or better in His service, than the human brain. Muhammed the Prophet (pbuh) was not an educated man, when he was chosen to be the last Messenger of G-d. And Allah said "We revealed it upon his heart."

If He, Allah, had revealed that weighty Book upon the brain of the uneducated Muhammed (pbuh), it would have destroyed him. If He had revealed it upon a mountain, the mountain would have crumbled into dust. Praise be to Allah.

The focus now is on Ummatu Islamia, the International Community of Al-Islam. Allah says in the Qur'an of Abraham, Peace be upon him, that he is a community, not just an individual, not just a man. G-d blessed him as a community, and his community, G-d promised, would be the whole of mankind, all people.

Adam is the first leader and father of mankind, for man's human nature. Abraham is the first

بسم الله الرحمن الرحيم

Imam W. Deen Mohammed

leader and father of mankind for the intellect. And Muhammed the Prophet is a Prophet like Moses, according to G-d's Word in the Qur'an. And the order he has established is after the order of Prophet Abraham, upon them all be Peace. Abraham was a community. And Muhammed was given to the world as the leader of the believers to guide us into community life, so that we will be responsible for community life.

In congregation, every believer, no believer is excused, is obligated to learn how to lead the prayers, to lead not only him or herself but to lead a group in prayer. Both males and females are obligated to do that. That tells us very clearly that we are responsible not only for leading ourselves individually, but we are responsible for leading the group, the collective body, as well as the individuals. G-d says; "You are the best community evolved or brought out for the good of all people, for all mankind." It speaks to us in the plural, meaning every one of us. So how can we live Islam, live a Muslim life, and not feel the obligation to our fellow man, when G-d says He has brought us out of the world of darkness and ignorance and oppression and sins, etc., so that we will be of benefit, of service to all people? When Muhammed (pbuh) is a mercy to all the worlds?

Like our leader, Muhammed (pbuh), we also should have it in our hearts to be a mercy to all the worlds. We should want our community to be a model community. G-d wants us to be a witness for all of the communities. How are we going to be a witness for all of the communities, if we don't see our obligation to all people and to all other societies? That we build and establish a model society that will be a witness under G-d. That He has given man

Imam W. Deen Mohammed

the guidance to have the best society or best community life possible on this earth.

If we live it, we will be that model. It was done by Muhammed, the Prophet, Prayers and Peace be on him. He achieved that in his lifetime, and he left that to us. We are the inheritors of that great society that the last of the Prophets, the Seal of the Prophets, established. So we have to become more and more aware, more and more conscious of the fact that we have the superior guidance. And if we follow it, we will have the superior community life. None will have any community life to match ours, to compete with ours. If we pursue what G-d has given us through Muhammed the Prophet (pbuh), the Qur'an, as guidance and follow his methods, his principles, respect his character, we will have the best. "And obey G-d and obey His Messenger." This is the answer.

BUILD & ESTABLISH A MODEL SOCIETY

This religion is not difficult. This religion is very clear. You don't have to be a scientist or a mathematician or a psychologist or a great philosopher or the high-minded person living in the skies because the earth is too small for you. You don't have to be that kind of person to learn this religion, to practice this religion and contribute to the success of the Muslim life on this planet. This religion will make you a special brain.

I was not a special brain. My father had no education; he went no further than three years of elementary school in Sandersville, Georgia in the South. He told us that he had to teach himself how to write a good hand. He educated himself. And when his teacher came along, Mr. Fard, he inspired my father to want bigger and greater things. Mr. Fard made him a higher student and a more broad-minded student than he was before, struggling to write a good letter,

بسم الله الرحمن الرحيم

Imam W. Deen Mohammed

and the man became a genius. The challenge that my father was given by his teacher, challenged his mind and brought out the genius in that man who didn't have good circumstances in the South and in the North.

I remember the Hon. Elijah Muhammad saying many times in the Temple, "When you become a member here, you automatically become a member of every Islamic nation." No matter what we thought of what he was saying and doing, we have to admit that the Hon. Elijah Muhammad was sensitizing us to be united with all Muslims on this planet. And thanks be to Allah, it has happened.

We now are part of the international Ummah, out of the United States of America. Our obligation here is to work with all that we have, fearing G-d, loving G-d and seeking G-d for forgiveness of our shortcomings, of our sins, and asking Him for Mercy and Guidance. It is not just for me, but also for my children to come, for my brother's children to come, for my loved ones and my friends and for the whole of mankind. It is for every human person on this earth.

That is what is in my heart and stays in my heart. That is what drives me to want to do more and more and reach wider and wider areas of understanding, of knowledge, but also of opportunity to contribute to the betterment of my neighborhood, of my community, of my city, of my state, my country and the whole world.

We don't have to have one hundred percent of us with that strong motivation moving us every time we wake up and go to bed. We only need a very few people like that, to keep the right thing on the rest of our minds and to keep us going forward in the path of G-d. And G-d

بسم الله الرحمن الرحيم

Imam W. Deen Mohammed

says, "Strive in His Path with your wealth and with your own souls, your own selves." The poor man may think that he is not being spoken to, but he is. You may not have wealth in the terms of U.S. currency or of some other currency, but if you have a strong moral constitution, then you represent a wealth of resources in terms of moral life and moral influence. And you are supposed to spend of your own soul. So you can't go into your pocket, but G-d says to spend of your own soul. If you have these qualities, these riches in your own soul, then share them with others.

Muhammed the Prophet (pbuh) said we are obligated to fight against injustice, against wrong. He said the first and the best fight is to fight with your hands; that means to get involved physically. And if you can't find the wherewithal or circumstances won't permit you to do that, he said, then do it with your tongue,

BUILD & ESTABLISH A MODEL SOCIETY

to speak out against the wrong. Sometimes you can't speak out against it, because you may lose your life and your wife and children will be killed, your house and whole family burned up. Sometimes, there are some extreme conditions in the world.

So we are allowed to save our lives, not to speak out when you know you are going to get killed. Then it says, at least have it in your heart to dislike what is going on. Let your soul and heart be opposed to what is going on. This is a very sensible religion. It is a good sense religion, a religion for the best of the human nature. It is the religion of the origin of human beings, of the pattern or order or form of human life that He evolved man upon.

Man evolved and progressed upon the purity of the original nature that G-d created for him. It was that nature that made him want to know, Why? Why is it this way? Why is the sky as it

بسم الله الرحمن الرحيم

Imam W. Deen Mohammed

is? Why does the sun rise on time and repeats the rising, and I get up for work and the night comes on time and makes me sleepy? That is how the thinkers and philosophers were born. They wanted to know, why? That is the original nature given to them by their Creator, G-d. The original nature of the human being is what G-d patterned the whole of mankind upon. If the Turks became great people, if the Irish became great people, if the Chinese became great people, if the Africans or whomever became great people, it was firstly because G-d created them as a special, precious, rich, resourceful vessel with all of those possibilities there.

If they followed the best of their human aspirations, then they gave birth to leaders who led them into great heights of society and civilization and the sciences. Allah wants us to think rationally. Allah wants us to think with respect for His creation and the laws of His creation, so that we will gain great knowledge and sciences from His creation and get His Second Mercy, the Mercy that He says will give us comfort. "And He has expanded or extended everything for knowledge and mercy." The sentence in the Arabic is so exact in its expression; it would take a lecture alone to explain what that is saying.

Allah is saying to us that if we get the science that is in His creation, it will make your life more comfortable and that will be His Compassion on you. That is His greatest Mercy, His greatest Compassion on you; that He gives you His sciences that He puts in His creation. In the winter you can be warm, and in the summer you can be cool. And you can travel without hardship. Isn't that mercy, love, compassion? But man gets it and then gives himself the credit.

بسم الله الرحمن الرحيم

Imam W. Deen Mohammed

Although man will make the computer and still give himself the credit, not the computer… although the computer is doing wonders and running the factory and guiding the plane. He doesn't say, "Thank the computer." He says, "Thank me, for I created it." Well, he should thank Allah for creating the computer in his head. Know that man is not the creator of that computer, Allah is. Man could not even find anything to put in his computer, until G-d created it.

Praise be to Allah, "You are the best of the society or community brought out or evolved for the good of all people." We have to now be aware that we are again beginning to grow in business establishment. The material world is a test, like many other things. It is a test for our spiritual life. It is a material world and it will deceive us. It will take our souls on the path to greed and selfishness and arrogance of power,

BUILD & ESTABLISH A MODEL SOCIETY

if we don't obey the guidance of G-d and follow the human model that He wants us to be.

Understand that we got our first and great start from the teacher Fard, and his student, Elijah Poole Muhammad. Great wisdom was put in the language that he left with us, and thank Allah, his son was blessed to find it. Now again, we are coming into business, and we will be tested like we were tested before, but this time we won't fail. I have assurance in my soul, heart and mind that this time we will not fail. We are going to grow bigger and bigger and bigger in business.

The motivation is the same as it was then. Do you think the Hon. Elijah Muhammad wanted you to support business so he could ride around in fine cars and live in luxury? No, he did not. I know him better than that, and my brothers and sisters know him better than that. And you who knew him personally knew him

Imam W. Deen Mohammed

better than that. He wanted to see us have a better life, a better future, that we have the promise of good homes, plenty money and friendships in all walks of life.

How can you have friendships in all walks of life with plenty money, if you are a crook or a criminal? You will have plenty money, but you won't have friendships in all walks of life. That tells us that the Hon. Elijah Muhammad wanted us to be decent, upright, honorable people. Not materialistic, greedy for money. He wanted to meet our needs or necessities to have better Islamic schools, better Mosques, Muslim places of worship, and better material environments for our elderly and young children, for our wives bearing our children. A man should never think of having a house for himself before he thinks of having a house for his wife who is going to bear his children.

BUILD & ESTABLISH A MODEL SOCIETY

We are a people who think about community first, and the first community is the community of family. That is what Allah, G-d, wants us to do, take care of our families and feel for the brother and his family. Let your charity go outside of your own family and help somebody else. That is what Allah wants for us. This is a simple religion.

We are challenged again, and it is no different than what it was before. The challenge under my father was jealousy, envy, selfishness, resenting that someone else has a few dollars more than you, resenting that someone else has a position bigger than yours with more prestige. The same old things that brought nations and ancient people down were in the Nation of Islam and are here now. It never changes. The excellence of the people stays, and the cancer that was in the people stays.

بسم الله الرحمن الرحيم

Imam W. Deen Mohammed

Some people don't care about material things. They get material things only so they can have power. If they can get power without getting material things, they will do it that way. They will be bickering and arguing and undermining each other. We have to work for business. We have to work for the cause. We have to see our life as Muslims more important than everything else.

I hear this expression, "I love this community." How can you love this community, if you don't love me? How can you love this community, and you don't support me? That is a liar who does not love this community. It makes that person burn inside when they see me go up and people loving and admiring me. If you loved the community, you will love the person who is helping the community and making a contribution to the community.

BUILD & ESTABLISH A MODEL SOCIETY

You aren't going to love someone who is giving the community nothing but mosquito bites and bad air. How can you love those who are doing nothing and not love those who are doing something? How much are you giving to the community? Or are you just living on it like a leach. Brothers, your obligation is that you be a soldier and know the imposter among you. Know that he is not a soldier.

If he is always talking community and not giving anything to it, that is the imposter, the devil among you, the snake in the grass. If you love your leader, how can you undermine my best help? It is like you are cutting away my right arm. This is not going to be easy. It is never easy to do something big. Community life is a big undertaking. It is a big challenge to establish your own community life and have your own selves responsible for it.

Imam W. Deen Mohammed

Don't think the devil, and greedy ones influenced by the devil, aren't going to be eyeing what we are doing and see how they can capitalize on what we are doing for their own benefit. They want to see how they can cipher something off for themselves. They want to see how they can turn the tables from what we want to have on the table to what they want to have on the table. This is no small challenge.

G-d has chosen us to be responsible for community life. Everywhere in this world, no matter what nation we are in and whether the circumstances will permit them to do it or not, they should at least have it in their hearts to build a model of how G-d wants man to live on this planet.

We thank you and we thank G-d. We ask Him for His Forgiveness and for His Mercy and Guidance.

بسم الله الرحمن الرحيم

ABOUT IMAM W DEEN MOHAMMED

Imam W. Deen Mohammed was unanimously elected as leader of his community after the passing of his father in 1975; the Honorable Elijah Muhammad, founder, leader, and builder of the Nation of Islam.

At a very early age, Imam Mohammed developed a keen scholastic interest in science, psychology and religion. He began his education, from elementary through secondary school, at the University of Islam in Chicago. Further educational pursuits took him to Wilson Junior College, where he concentrated on microbiology and to the Loop Junior College where he studied English, history, and the social sciences. However, his primary education has come from self-study and

BUILD & ESTABLISH A MODEL SOCIETY

through his continued pursuit of religion and social truths.

Imam Mohammed's astute leadership, profound social commentary on major issues, piercing scriptural insight into the Torah, Bible and Quran, and his unique ability to apply scriptural interpretation to social issues have brought him numerous awards and high honors. He is a man of vision who has performed many historical firsts.

In 1992, he delivered the first invocation in the U.S. senate to be given by a Muslim. In 1993 he gave an Islamic prayer at President William Jefferson Clinton's first inaugural interfaith prayer service, and again in 1997 at President Clinton's second inaugural interfaith prayer service. His strong interest in interfaith dialogue led him to address the Muslim-Jewish conference on March 6, 1995, with leaders of

بسم الله الرحمن الرحيم

Imam W. Deen Mohammed

Islam and Reform Judaism in Glencoe, IL. In October of 1996, Imam Mohammed met Pope John Paul, II, at the Vatican, at the invitation of Archbishop William Cardinal Keeler and the Focolare Movement. He met with the Pope again, on October 28, 1999, on the "Eve of the New Millennium" in St. Peter's basilica with many other world religious leaders.

In 1997, the Focolare Movement presented him with the "Luminosa Award," for promoting interfaith dialogue, peace, and understanding in the U.S. In 1999, Imam Mohammed served on the advisory panel for Religious Freedom Abroad, formed by Secretary of State Madeline Albright. He assisted in promoting religious freedom in the United States and abroad. In April, 2005, Imam Mohammed participated in a program that featured, "a conversation with Imam W. Deen Mohammed and Cardinal George of the Catholic Archdiocese."

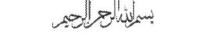

There are many more accolades, achievements and accomplishments made by Imam W. Deen Mohammed. His honorary Doctorates, Mayoral, and Gubernatorial Proclamations give testament to his recognized voice, and the benefit of his leadership to Muslims and non-Muslims alike. He was appointed to the World Supreme Council of Mosques because of the value of his work and leadership in America.

Today, the dignity and world recognition Imam Mohammed has generated is seen all across the world.

بسم الله الرحمن الرحيم

Imam W. Deen Mohammed

OTHER TITLES BY IMAM W. DEEN MOHAMMED
Contact WDM Publications for availability

- The Schemes of Satan the Enemy of Man
- Noah's Flood Lecture Series
- Ramadan: Meaning, Blessings, Celebration
- Muslim Unity
- Healthy Consciousness in Society
- Diversity in Al Islam
- Mohammed The Prophet ﷺ | The Perfect Man - The Complete Man
- The Story of Joseph
- And Follow the Best Thereof
- It's Time We Sing A New Song [75 Select Poems]
- Wake Up to Human Life
- Islam The Religion of Peace
- As the Light Shineth From the East
- Life the Final Battlefield

بسم الله الرحمن الرحيم

BUILD & ESTABLISH A MODEL SOCIETY

- Message of Concern [Removal of All Images That Attempt to Portray Divine]
- The Teachings of W. D. Muhammad 1975
- The Lectures of Imam W. D. Muhammad 1976
- Book of Muslim Names
- The Man and the Woman in Islam
- Prayer and Al-Islam
- Religion on the Line
- Imam W. Deen Muhammad Speaks from Harlem, N.Y. Book 1
- Imam W. Deen Muhammad speaks from Harlem, N.Y.: Challenges That Face Man Today Book 2
- Meeting the Challenge: Halal Foods for Our Everyday Needs
- An African American Genesis
- Focus on Al-Islam: Interviews with Imam W. Deen Mohammed
- Al-Islam: Unity, and Leadership
- Worst Oppression Is False Worship "The Key Is Tautened-Oneness of Allah

بسم الله الرحمن الرحيم

Imam W. Deen Mohammed

- Growth for a Model Community in America
- Islam's Climate for Business Success
- Mohammed Speaks
- Blessed Ramadan - The Fast of Ramadan
- Plans for a Better Future: Peace, Inclusion and International Brotherhood
- The Champion We Have in Common: The Dynamic African American Soul
- A Time for Greater Communities Vol. 1-4
- Securing our Share of Freedom
- Return to Innocence: Transitioning of the Nation of Islam

بسم الله الرحمن الرحيم

BUILD & ESTABLISH A MODEL SOCIETY

Purchase Copies of This Publication:

WDM Publications
PO Box 1944, Calumet City, IL 60409

Phone: 708-862-7733
Email: wdmpublications@sbcglobal.net

www.WDMPublications.com

For More on Imam W. Deen Mohammed

Ministry of Imam W. Deen Mohammed
PO Box 1061, Calumet City, IL 60409

Phone: 708-679-1587
Email: wdmministry@sbcglobal.net

www.TheMosqueCares.com

Made in the USA
Middletown, DE
03 February 2024